Fashion through the Ag

Shoes & Boots

ticktock

First published in Great Britain in 2006 by ticktock Media Ltd.,
Unit 2, Orchard Business Centre, North Farm Road,
Tunbridge Wells, Kent, TN2 3XF
ISBN1 86007 980 6
Printed in China
A CIP catalogue record for this book is available from the British Library.

Picture credits

t=top, b=bottom, c=centre, l-left, r=right

Corbis: 16b, 17t, 27b. Fort Rock Museum: 6b. Werner Forman Archve: 7t, 8-9 all, 10-11 all, 12-13 all, 20-21c, 21r. Yorvik Museum: 14l.

Every effort has been made to trace the copyright holders, and we apologise in advance for any unintentional omissions. We would be pleased to insert the appropriate acknowledgements in any subsequent edition of this publication.

CONTENTS

- *Glossary terms are boldened on first use on each spread*

INTRODUCTION

Humans are the only animals to design and make footwear. Why do we choose to wear coverings on our feet? Boots and shoes have a practical purpose; they keep us warm and dry and protect our skin from cuts and scratches. But they also change the way we look, and send messages about us to people we meet.

The early ancestors of modern humans left footprints behind at Olduvai Gorge in Tanzania, Africa. This illustration is based on fossil finds.

Barefoot history

Shoes, boots, socks and sandals are all recent inventions. For millions of years, men, women and children walked barefoot, like animals and the soles of their feet hardened to cope. Later migration to colder climates necessitated the wearing of shoes.

How many different materials have been used to make shoes?

At least ten: bark, grass, wood, hide, fur, cloth, silk, rubber, plastic, metal.

Sports footwear

For 2,000 years – maybe more – special footwear has been designed for sports and exciting outdoor pastimes. Sports footwear gives support to players' feet and ankles. It also helps them move faster.

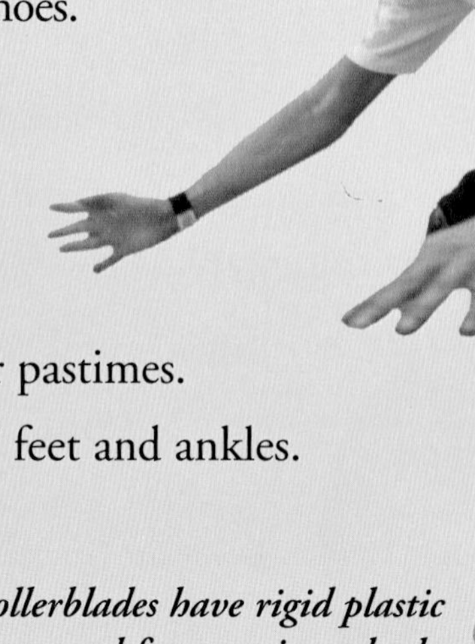

Rollerblades have rigid plastic boots and fast-turning wheels.

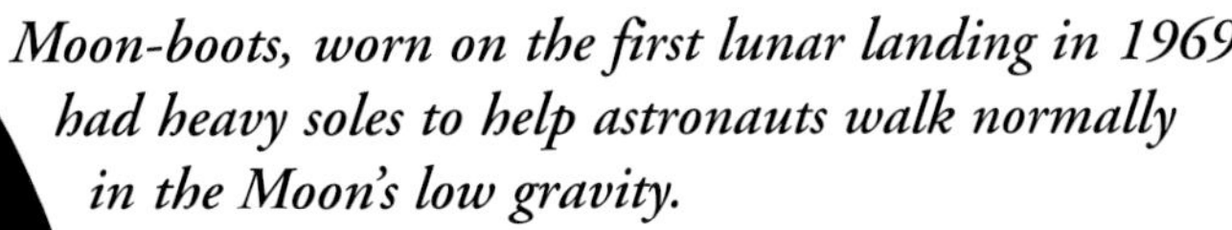

Moon-boots, worn on the first lunar landing in 1969, had heavy soles to help astronauts walk normally in the Moon's low gravity.

Extreme footwear

In the late 20th century, new kinds of footwear were designed for extreme environments. These included blazing fires, undersea exploration, and the surface of the Moon, where heavy boots helped keep the astronaut grounded by countering the effects of the Moon's gravity.

Flattering footwear

Heels on boots and shoes increase the wearer's height and make the legs look longer. They also throw the body out of balance, creating a swaying, forward-tilting walk. In women, this emphasises **erogenous** (sexually attractive) areas, especially the bosom and the hips.

Over a third of women wear high heels to improve the appearance of their legs.

THE FIRST SHOES

Footwear was not invented until late in human history. The first shoes or boots were probably made between 50,000 BC - 20,000 BC. The oldest known image of people wearing foot-coverings comes from a rock-painting in Spain, made around 15,000 years ago.

Skins and fibres

The first footwear was made of the same materials as other early clothing: animal skins and plant fibres. Strips of **hide** or fur were wrapped around the feet and lower legs and held in place by rawhide laces. In cold climates, they kept wearers warm. Plant fibres, such as **bark** and dried grass, were twisted together to make simple sandals. These protected feet from thorns, stones, biting insects and burning sand in hot climates.

Traditional sandals made from plant fibres by Aboriginal people in Australia still follow very ancient designs.

Woven soles

By around 10,000 BC, footwear design hade become more sophisticated. Soles for sandals were woven to fit the precise shape of the foot, and were fastened over the **instep** and around the ankle by neat strings of twisted plant-fibre.

The oldest surviving footwear so far discovered was a pair of pre-contact sandals found at Fort Rock, Oregon, USA, dating from between 10,500 BC -9,300 BC.

Bear-skin and deer-skin boots (left) with grass and net padding (above) found on the frozen body of 'Utzi', a man who died in the mountains of Italy around 3,300 BC.

Laces and insulation

The first **laced** shoes were made at least 7,000 years ago. They consisted of a piece of animal hide pierced with holes around the edge. A thin lace (strip) of raw-hide was threaded through holes, then pulled tight to gather the shoe around the foot. By around 3,500 BC, boots were made with separate soles and uppers.

How did the Fort Rock shoes survive so long?

They were buried under ash from an erupting volcano.

Knee high

The first boots covered only the feet and ankles. They were worn with **leggings** that had a special flap attached. This extended to cover the top part of the foot and could be tucked inside the boot lacing. But by around 1,000 BC, high boots were made by joining leggings, **sole** and uppers together. These covered the feet and all the lower leg as far as the knee.

*Lifelike **terracotta** (baked clay) statues of warriors wearing high boots guard the tomb of Qin Shi Huangdi, the first Emperor of China, who died in 206 BC.*

ANCIENT EGYPT AND ITS NEIGHBOURS

In many early societies, like Ancient Egypt, footwear was a sign of status. Only rich people could afford to purchase shoes or sandals and only royal or noble families were allowed to wear them all the time.

These Egyptian men are not wearing any shoes while baking bread. This was usual practise in ancient Egypt.

Going barefoot

Most ordinary Egyptian men, and all Egyptian women, went barefoot both inside and outside. In the hot, dry climate of Egypt, their feet did not get wet or cold, but they did get cut, bruised, dusty and dirty. Egyptian medical texts contain many remedies for sore, aching feet.

A Pharaoh's footwear

The Ancient Egyptians buried their Pharaohs (kings) and nobles in magnificent tombs, with everything they would need in the **afterlife**, including carvings. Sandals were the most common footwear design. Most had a flat sole, **toe-post** and wide straps over the **instep** or round the heel. A Pharaoh's might be made of gold.

Who wore high heels in Ancient Egypt?

Slaughter-house workers, so their feet would not touch the blood from animals.

This gold statue of Pharaoh Tutankhamun shows him wearing typical Ancient Egyptian sandals. Pharaohs' sandals were often decorated with real gold and precious stones.

An expert trade

Egyptian sandals were made by expert craft-workers. They used a wide variety of materials, including wood, **palm**-fronds, burlap cloth and plaited **papyrus** (reeds that grew beside the River Nile). They were also some of the first people to use **tanned** leather.

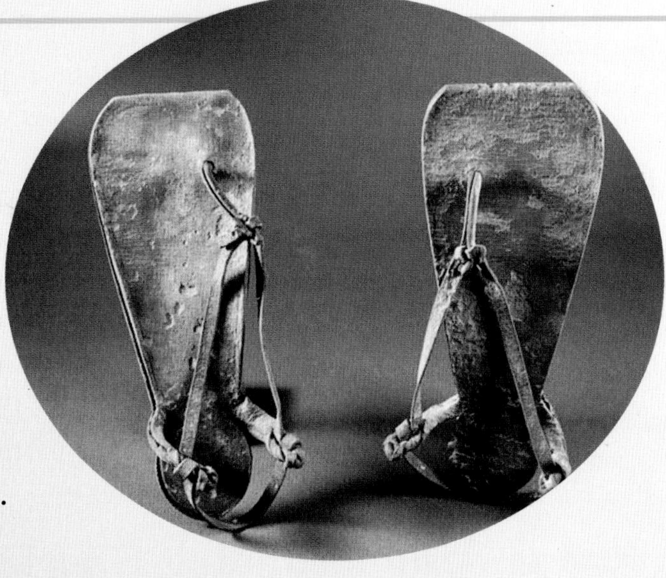

*Egyptian tanned **leather** sandals made around 3,000 BC.*

Climbing and riding

Neighbouring West Asian peoples had to survive in high mountains and cold weather. So they developed footwear that was suitable for climbing up steep, snowy paths, or for riding long distances. Hittite mountain villagers (who lived in Turkey around 2000 BC) made tough ankle boots with turned-up toes.

Clay model of a Hittite boot, made around 2,000 BC.

ANCIENT GREECE AND ITS NEIGHBOURS

The Ancient Greek homeland bordered the Mediterranean Sea, and ships from many European and West Asian civilisations called at Greek ports. Greek travellers and traders learned leather-working and shoe-making technologies from neighbouring peoples.

A marble female foot dressed in a sandal, dating from 1st-2nd century AD.

Female fashions

Greek footwear was made from soft leather, smoothed and polished with pork fat or olive oil. It was often brightly coloured with plant-dyes. For women, fashionable styles included slippers, open-toed shoes, **mules** (shoes without heel-backs), shoes with thick cork soles and sandals.

Styles for men

Greek men also wore sandals. But for long journeys, they put on walking shoes with thick, **hobnailed** soles, or short lace-up boots that protected the foot and gave extra support to the ankles.

Where did our word 'sandal' originate?

In Ancient Greece, 'Sandalia' was the Greek word for a wooden, leather or woven grass sole

This statue of Asclepius, the Greek god of medicine, shows him wearing sturdy ankle boots with thick soles and open toes.

Rough country

In wartime, Greek warriors protected their legs with curved **greaves** (shin-plates). These were made of metal (for rich men) or (for ordinary soldiers) thick boiled leather. They fastened behind the leg with **leather** straps and buckles, and were worn with short lace-up boots or heavy sandals.

A modern reproduction of Ancient Greek greaves.

Enemy styles

Greek city-states often fought among themselves. But they joined together to fight foreign enemies, especially the Persians, who ruled an empire based in the land now known as Iran. The Persians wore different clothing and footwear from the Greeks. Their usual footwear was short, ankle-length boots.

Persian noblemen and satraps (government ministers) carved on the walls of the royal palace at Persepolis, Iran, around 500 BC.

THE ANCIENT ROMAN EMPIRE

The Ancient Romans lived in Italy. At the peak of Roman power, around AD 100, their capital city, Rome, housed over a million people. City inhabitants included expert shoemakers. They invented shoes designed to fit right or left feet only.

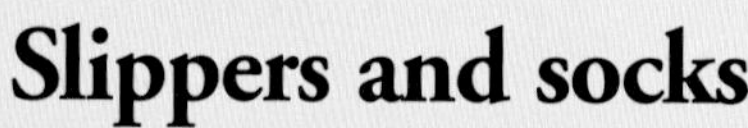

Slippers and socks

Romans were also some of the first people in the world to wear socks, called 'udones'. These were pairs of boot-shapes cut out of tightly-woven fabric, then carefully stitched together. **Udones** might be worn by themselves indoors, or out of doors, for warmth, with boots or sandals.

What did the Romans use to dye leather shoes red?

The outer rinds of pomegranates, dried and imported from Asia.

A bronze statue of a lower leg, clothed in a woven woollen sock and a simple sandal.

Caligae and Calcaei

For outdoor wear, the most important foot coverings were **caligae** (shoes or boots with thick, hobnailed, soles made of many layers of leather) and **calcaei** (flat leather shoes, shaped like ballet slippers. Calcaei could only be worn by high-ranking Romans.

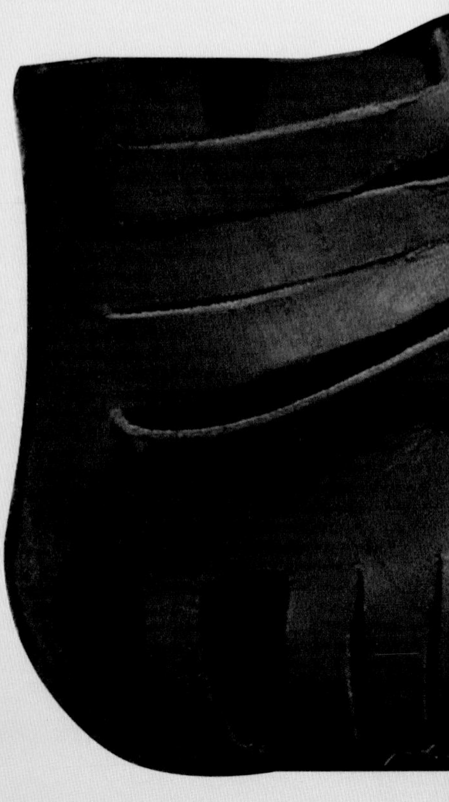

This modern reproduction of a Roman caliga shows its thick sole.

This Roman soldier wears calf-high army boots with the toes left exposed.

Soldiers' sandals

Roman sandals could be lightweight – just a thin **sole** with slender straps – or heavy versions of calf-high army boots with the toes left open. Egyptian-style sandals, made of plaited **palm** fronts, were mostly worn by actors. But they were also worn by priests and philosophers, as a sign of humility.

Eastern influences

As Roman power collapsed, Roman fashions were influenced by designs copied from neighbouring peoples. The Byzantines, who ruled the eastern half of the Roman empire from around AD 330 wore ankle-boots or soft cloth and **leather** shoes with turned-up toes, copied from West Asian peoples.

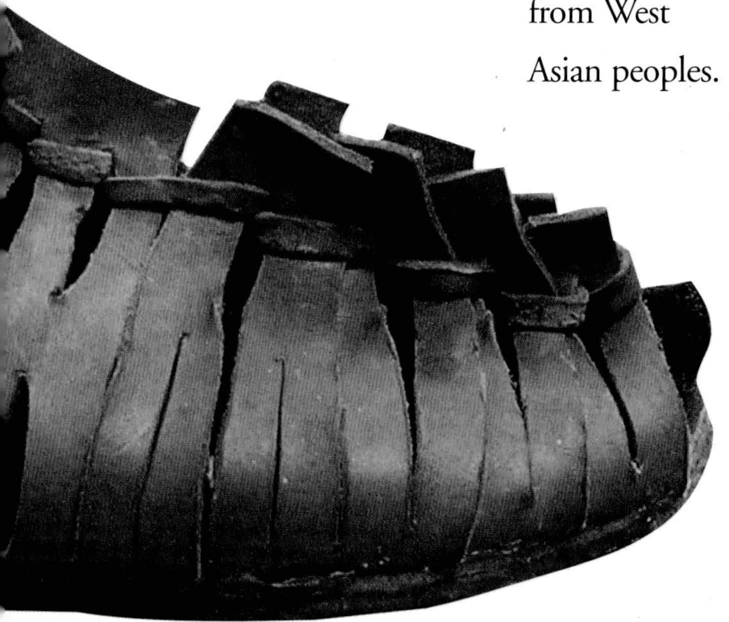

This 4th century statue shows a group of embracing emperors represents the four leaders of the crumbling Roman Empire.

MEDIEVAL EUROPE

In medieval Europe, ancient shoe-making traditions survived for centuries. In the far north, Viking people continued to wear fur-lined boots. In the far south, some people wore Roman-style sandals. But as well as these old styles, many new footwear fashions developed.

Viking footwear

Throughout Europe, most men and women wore new-style shoes that covered the whole foot to just below the ankle. These were convenient to wear with trousers, or with long, full skirts. They slipped easily on and off, and fastened by means of a flap at one side secured by leather ties, or a wooden toggle.

Leather shoe, with flap fastening, found in the Viking city of York, England. It dates from around AD 850.

Shoes for war

During the early medieval period, soldiers wore their own, everyday footwear in battle. But in later years, wealthy knights, from noble families, paid for tailor-made suits of armour, to protect them from head to toe.

Leg Protection

How long were the points on medieval men's shoes?

6 inches.

Ordinary men and women, who worked on the land, needed protection from cold and damp, and from rough vegetation. They could not afford socks, or high **leather** boots that reached to the knee. So they wore simple flat shoes, and protected their lower legs with bands of cloth or sheep-skin.

This medieval suit of armour features shoes called sabatons.

Garters tied crossways round trouser-legs helped block draughts.

High fashion

Wealthy men and women wore many different styles of fine leather shoes, with shapes that changed over the centuries. Many popular designs had long, pointed toes, stuffed with sheep's wool for stiffening. By around 1400, fine shoes worn outside the home were protected by '**pattens**' – thick over-shoes, rather like clogs, made of wood and leather.

*Young man's fashion shoe, made around AD 1400, from fine, soft leather by expert '**cordwainers**' (leatherworkers).*

EASTERN REGIONS

The peoples of Asia created many different kinds of footwear. Designs were shaped by local climates, and by available materials. Wars, invasions and migrations also brought changes of footwear.

*These traditional toe-post' sandals have wooden soles and **leather** straps.*

Simple sandals

In hot tropical regions, for example, South-East Asia, many people went barefoot or wore simple, lightweight sandals. These were made of wood, leather or plaited plant fibres. Typically, they had straps running along each side of the foot from a small 'post' in between the toes.

The Mughal dynasty, who ruled north India from 1526 to 1858, were descended from Mongol princes. This painting shows typical Central-Asian style boots.

Central Asian boots

In many parts of East Asia, outdoor footwear styles were based on soft **leather** ankle boots worn by nomads who rode on horseback across grassy steppes. From around AD 1200 – 1500 these styles were carried over a vast area, from China to India and Russia, by armies of Mongol invaders. Indoors, men and women went barefoot, or wore backless slippers. These were also popular in West Asia.

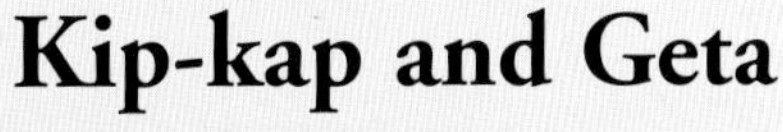

Kip-kap and Geta

For protection from rain, or from rubbish in the streets, women in many parts of Asia wore **clogs** with thick wooden soles that raised their feet at least 5 cm/2 inches above dirty ground. These clogs often had names that echoed the sound the wearer made as she clattered along. In Turkey they were called **'kip-kap'** (or 'kub-kob'), in Japan 'geta'.

*This Japanese woman and her servant girl wear wooden **geta** clogs with 'tabi' (socks that have a separate space for the big toe).*

Who invented the first non-slip footwear?

Poet Xie Lingyin, around 350 BC.

Working Shoes and Lily Feet

From around AD 900, the custom of foot-binding spread among noble families in China. Young girls' feet were gradually bent then tightly bandaged to create a 'lily' shape. Tiny shoes (see below), often beautifully embroidered, were made to fit.

For almost 1000 years, 'lily feet' were a sign of high rank and beauty, but they made walking difficult and very painful.

AFRICA

In many parts of southern Africa, ordinary men and women did not wear shoes. From childhood, they went barefoot. Their feet became very strong, but they were in danger of injury from sharp stones, spiky plants, snakes and stinging insects.

Sandals from Tanzania, Africa.

Sandals for safety

Simple sandals, consisting of a flat **sole** fastened to the foot with straps or ties, gave protection from underfoot dangers. Most were made of **tanned** (treated) **leather** or raw-hide. Sandals, shape depended on local fashions flat and wide in West Africa, rounded and curved in Eastern regions. But they usually fastened with leather strips across the instep, round the back of the heel, and, sometimes, over the big toe. The finest sandals were decorated with brightly-coloured patterns painted on the leather.

Wooden clogs from Tanzania.

Rainforest clogs

In equatorial Africa, and dry, desert regions, such as the Horn of Africa (in the north-east) sheep and cattle do not thrive. So leather was not easily available for making sandals or shoes, and caftworkers made footwear from wood, instead. African **clogs** featured a thick flat sole, decorated with carved patterns, plus a **toe-post** topped by a wooden ball. This helped wearers keep the clogs on their feet; it was too wide to slip accidentally between their toes.

Camel-boots and slippers

In North Africa, good foot protection was needed when walking over hot sand, or riding camels through the desert. Many North African men and women wore flat, backless slippers, influenced by Middle Eastern designs. They removed them before entering their homes, or since most were Muslims before going into a mosque to say prayers. Desert nomads wore calf-length boots for long journeys on camels. These boots had thick leather soles but legs of colourful woollen fabric, woven by Tuareg women.

What other materials were used for making African footwear?

Plaited grass and - in Cameroon - cast metal.

A modern Œbabouche (North African backless slipper).

Fit for a king

Footwear was expensive, and therefore became a status symbol. It also featured in several traditional rituals. For example, kings of the Asante people (now of Ghana, West Africa) were never meant to set foot on the ground. They were too important and too holy. They were carried everywhere by there servants, and their feet were protected by special shoes. Other West African rulers, such as kings of the Yoruba people (now of Nigeria) also wore fancy footwear, as signs of their special status.

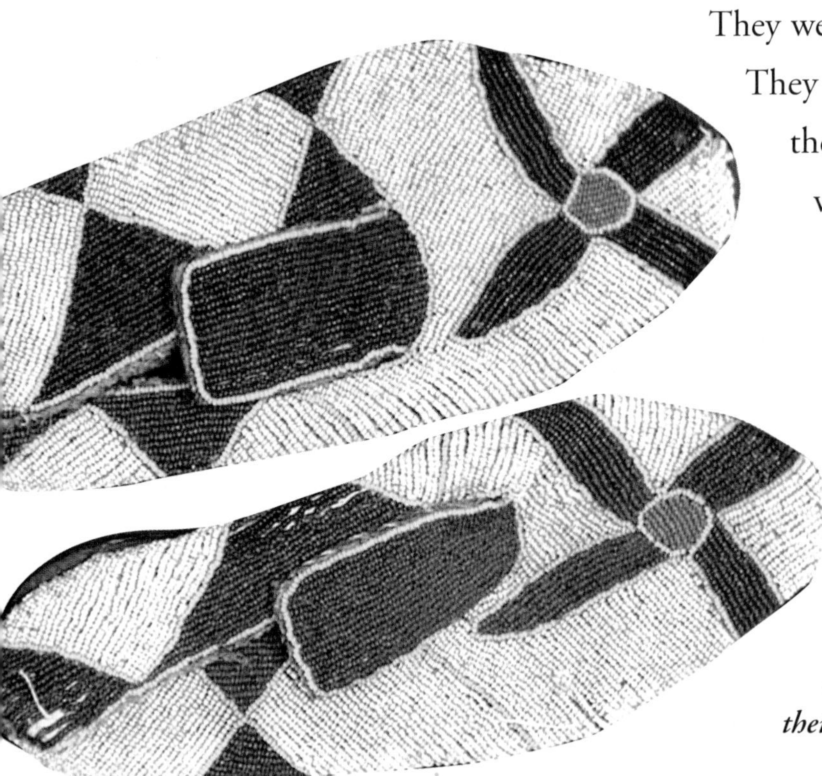

Yoruba royal boots and shoes were richly decorated with coloured beads that covered their entire surface.

THE AMERICAS

The continents of North and South America provide some of the most extreme and varied environments on Earth. The Native peoples who lived there developed many different kinds of footwear, made from local materials.

Gold and feathers

In South America, the Inca peoples of the Andes mountains made boots of llama skin for protection against the cold. For Inca royalty, these might be covered with thin sheets of real silver or gold. Ordinary Aztec people went barefoot, or made sandals of cactus fibre. But Aztec warriors and nobles wore **leather** sandals decorated with feathers, and padded leather shin-guards in battle.

Aztec sandals fastened at the front of the foot with decorated laces.

Winter boots

Inuit and Aleut people lived in the far North of America, where the ground was frozen for most of the year, then boggy in the summer months. They made two different kinds of boots, plus indoor slippers of soft, furry hare-skin. Winter boots were made of caribou skin or seal skin, hair side outwards. This produced a non-slip sole. Summer boots were made of thinner caribou skin. They were sewn with tiny stitches pulled very tight, to create almost waterproof seams.

Men's boots, made in Alaska, have sealskin soles and reindeer skin uppers, and are decorated with seal intestine, dog-hair, and wolverine fur.

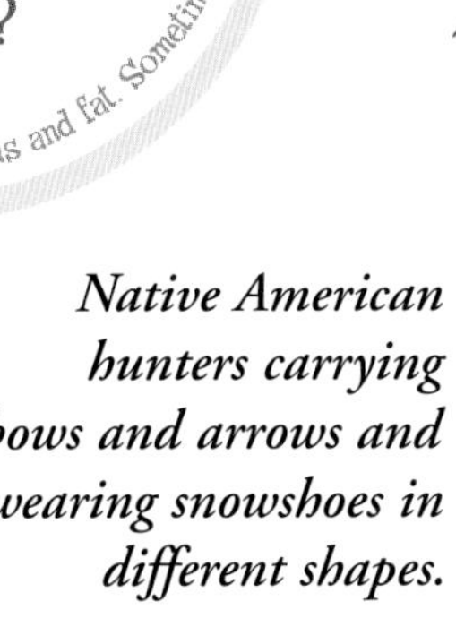

How did Native Americans prepare animal hide for making shoes?

They softened it by rubbing it with animal brains and fat. Sometimes, women chewed it.

Native American hunters carrying bows and arrows and wearing snowshoes in different shapes.

Walking on Snow

In the cold northern regions of North America, Native peoples made special shoes to allow them to hunt for food in the cold winter months, when deep snow covered the ground. Snow-shoes have frames of wood or antler, with sinews or thin strips of leather **laced** across them. They spread the wearer's weight over a much wider area than the **sole** of a human foot, and prevented him from sinking into the snow. Snow shoes are still used today.

Moccasins

In the woodlands and grasslands of North America, shoes called 'Makisin' (now: '**moccasins**') were made from single pieces of buckskin, gathered together around the top of the foot. The buck-skin was used hair side inwards, to create a warm lining. Dry grass might also be packed inside, for extra insulation. Sometimes a flap was added to cover the **upper** instep, plus a wide cuff around the ankle.

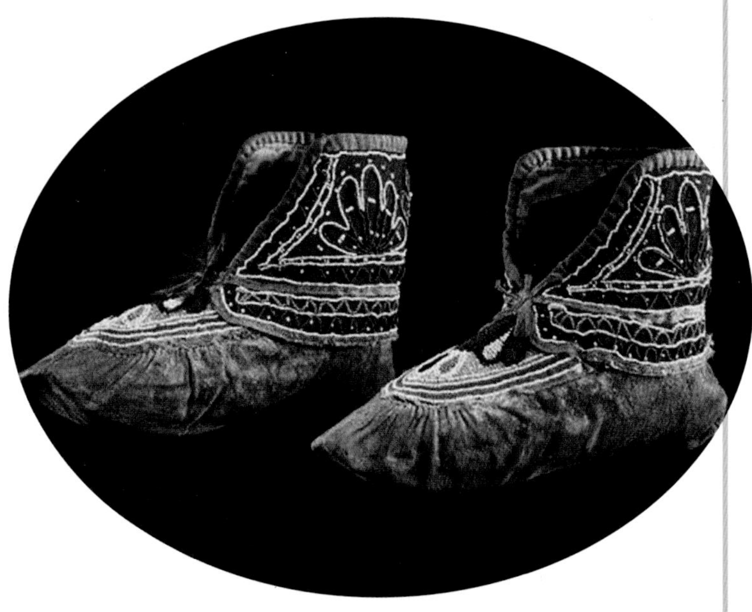

These 19th century moccasins were made to a traditional design. They are decorated with bright glass beads, obtained by trading with European settlers.

EUROPE 1500-1750

After around AD 1500, the gap grew greater between elaborate new styles, worn by rich, high ranking people, and rough, simple shoes, worn for work by ordinary men and women. Men's footwear designs were more extreme than women's, since women's shoes were hidden by long, full skirts.

Duck-bills

Medieval pointed shoes were replaced by shoes with extremely broad toes, nicknamed '**duck-bills**'. They were often made of fragile luxury materials, such as silk or velvet. In the early 16th, shoes might be **slashed**. This reflected high-fashion clothes worn by rich, powerful people.

King Henry VIII of England (reigned 1509-1547) shown wearing embroidered silk square-toed shoes.

Boots and spurs

For most of the 17th century, Europe was at war. Fashions reflected military styles, such as long **leather** boots with thick sturdy soles and turn-over, 'bucket' tops, originally designed to protect soldiers fighting on horseback. Underneath these tall boots, men wore over-the knee stockings, trimmed at the top with **lace** or fringing that was designed to be seen. High-ranking men added spurs, a sign that they were officers, or knights.

An elegant young man dressed in footwear popular at the English royal court around 1640.

High heels

After around 1650, high heels became popular for boots, shoes and slippers worn by men and women. Heels first became popular in France, but soon spread to many parts of Europe. Heeled footwear was made of leather, silk and velvet. It might be decorated with gold or silver buckles, large ribbon rosettes or bows, or jewels and embroidery.

This is a embroidered silk shoe (above) with a sloping 'French' heel.

How did 'French' heels get their name?

: They were made popular by several rulers of Franc who were of short stature.

Wooden clogs

Ordinary people could not afford high fashion footwear. Working men and women continued to wear plain ankle shoes, that had changed very little in design since the early Middle Ages. They also wore wooden **pattens**, or slip-on **clogs**. Both these styles were cheap, hard-working, and helped keep feet warm and dry when working on wet or frozen ground. With clogs, men and women wore thick knitted stockings, usually made from natural cream-coloured wool. Men sometimes also wore **gaiters** (shaped cloth leggings).

A couple from the Pyrenees Mountains in southern France. He is wearing traditional clogs; she wears plain, flat black-leather ankle shoes.

WESTERN WORLD 1750-1900

The years 1750-1900 saw great technical and economic changes, in Europe and the USA. New social groups developed: the working class and the middle class. Their lifestyles were reflected in their footwear.

This nineteenth-century cartoon shows the design of the first Wellington boots.

Boots for heroes

In 1776, the United States of America declared independence from Britain. To help fight back, the British hired brave troops from the Hesse region of Germany. These '**Hessian**' soldiers wore distinctive knee-high **leather** boots. In the USA, they developed into the heeled boots worn by cowboys. In Britain, they became the basis of tough, riding boots, first worn by army commander the Duke of **Wellington**.

Spatterdashes

Fine shoes were expensive, and very delicate. So, since the 1600s, men and women had covered their shoes and stockings up to the knee with thick, strong **leggings** called '**spatterdashes**' or '**gaiters**'. But by the 19th century, gaiters fell out of fashion. They were replaced by a short, ankle-length '**spat**' that filled the gap between the top of a shoe and the bottom of a trouser leg, or edge of a skirt hem.

Home Sweet Home

Middle-class families, who made their money from running businesses or working in the professions, placed great value on maintaining a spacious, comfortable, tranquil home. After returning home from work, men liked to relax in easy, backless slippers or house-shoes. These were made of soft fine leather, felted (boiled, compressed) wool, **tapestry**, or velvet.

A pair of 19th century gentleman's slippers, embroidered with gold stitching.

1750 – 1900

What were Wellington boots made of?

Polished leather. But waterproof rubber copies of them were made around 1856.

Sweet and simple

For most of the 19th century, shoes worn by fashionable women were light and delicate. Out of doors, they wore high-heeled ankle boots made of kid (baby-goat) leather, that fastened at the side with rows of tiny buttons. Indoors, they wore low-heeled slippers made of silk or fine leather.

This delicate fashionable footwear was a great contrast to the sturdy wooden **clogs** and **hobnailed** leather front-laced boots worn by working-class women.

This nineteenth-century woman's silk slipper was fastened by ribbons tied around the ankle.

Spats were made of stiffened fabric, in white (right), tan or grey. They buttoned neatly on one side, and were held in place by a buckled strap that passed under the instep.

WESTERN WORLD 1900-1950

The early 20th century was a troubled time. Millions of young men died in two World Wars (1914-1918 and 1939-1945); millions more families faced poverty, hunger and homelessness during the economic crises of the 1920s and 1930s. Many people felt lucky to have any shoes to wear; but fashions changed fast for the fortunate few.

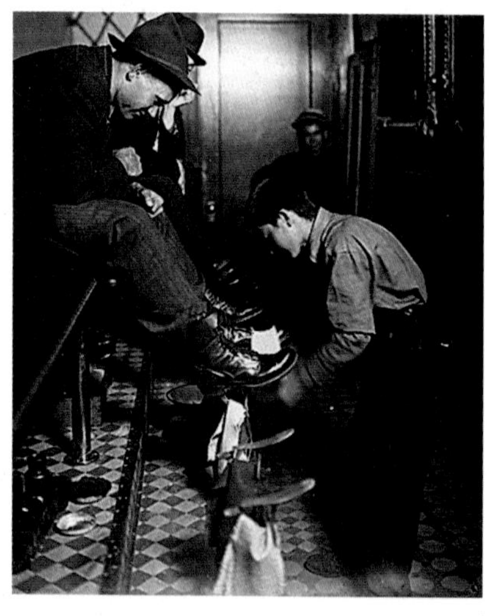

Jobless men and boys found work running shoe-shine stalls.

Functional footwear

At work and in wartime, ordinary men and women wore machine-made low-heeled, thick-soled, lace-up **leather** boots. Soldiers' boots were similar, but heavier and with **hobnailed** soles. Many people could not afford more than one pair of boots or shoes, so they looked after them carefully.

Short-skirt styles

Women's lives changed fast in the early 20th century. They won the vote, trained for careers, and took over men's work in wartime. They cut their hair and wore short skirts; for the first time for thousands of years, their legs were on display. Fashion shoes were designed to flatter. Popular styles had medium heels and tapering toes, and were held in place by a bar across the instep.

Short skirts and American-designed 't-bar' shoes were ideal for dancing.

Neat feet

Smart footwear was an essential part of the stylish, tailored look favoured by fashionable young men with money. In town, they wore polished '**Oxfords**'(neat **lace** up shoes).

These two-coloured 'co-respondent' shoes for men, made around 1930, are decorated with punched holes and zig-zag edging.

In the country, they wore boots or '**brogues**' (heavy **laced** shoes decorated with fancy stitching, punched hole patterns and tassels). In the USA, '**loafers**' (slip-on shoes) and '**co-respondent**' shoes (made with different coloured leathers) were fashionable.

How many nails did each British army boot have on its sole?

17.

Sports and leisure

At the start of the 20th century, men and women wore **laced** leather boots for outdoor sports such as football and cycling. For sports played indoors or in summer, such as basketball and tennis, they wore lighter shoes with canvas **uppers** and flexible, cushioned, rubber soles. In the USA, manufacturers created a whole new kind of footwear based on sportswear designs. These '**sneakers**' were comfortable and easy to wear, and became very popular with young people.

The 'Keds' brand of sneakers was launched in the USA in 1916. By the 1930s, as this shop window shows, there were many different styles.

WESTERN WORLD 1950-2000

Until the late 20th century, high fashion footwear was only worn by rich, privileged people. But mass media rapidly spread information about changing styles. And mass production methods made fashion footwear cheaper and more widely available than ever before.

'Bovver boots' – larger than life copies of traditional working boots – were worn by young men in Britain.

New meanings, old styles

New ways of working – in offices and automated factories – meant that heavy work boots were no longer required. Most men and women wore shoes. But exaggerated versions of traditional workers' styles became fashionable among young people, as a sign of rebellion. They were often made in bright colours or flimsy materials, as a joke or to mock authority. Hiking and combat boots were also popular but more practical.

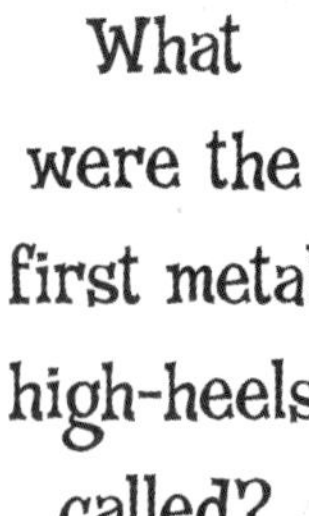

What were the first metal high-heels called?

Stilettos' (from an Italian word meaning 'thin, sharp knife').

High fashion

New footwear materials, such as metal and moulded plastic, made it possible for manufacturers to mass produce women's shoes with extremely thin, high heels. These caused an outrage when they first appeared in the 1960s. High heels can cause health problems such as shortened tendons and back problems, but despite this they remain popular. This pair dates from the 1990s.

Musician Ace Frehley of US glam-rock band 'Kiss' wears ghoulish stage make-up, a science fiction-style tunic, and amazing silver platform boots.

An everyday crown

Popular music performers discovered that an outrageous appearance on stage heightened their appeal. They commissioned artists, designers and other creative people to produce individual stage costumes.

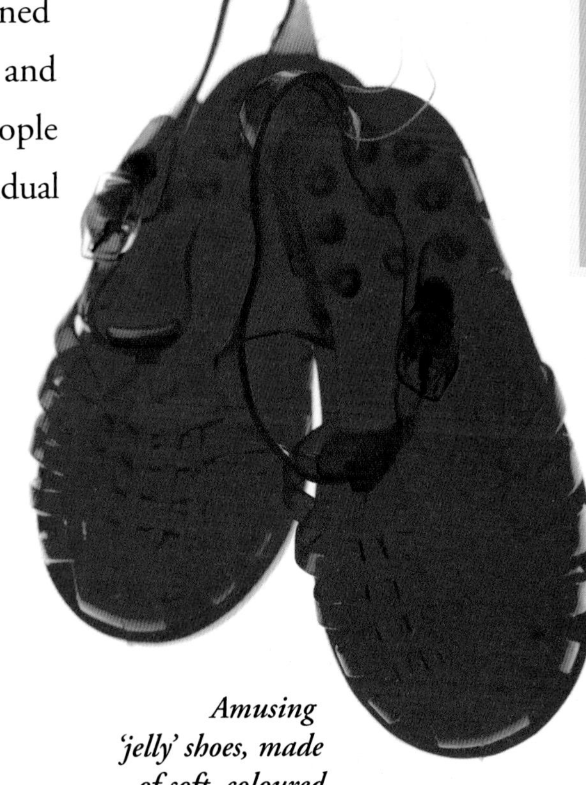

Amusing 'jelly' shoes, made of soft, coloured plastic, were first made by exclusive designers. But mass-produced versions, like these, were so cheap that they could be worn a few times, then thrown away.

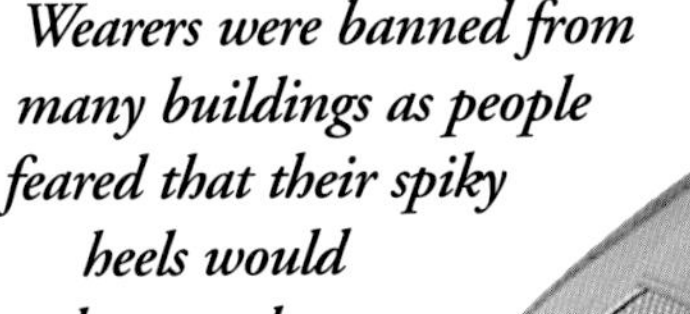

High heels caused an outrage when they first appeared. Wearers were banned from many buildings as people feared that their spiky heels would damage the floor.

Designer fashions

Top shoemakers were often inspired by science – such as the flat, square-toed **leather** 'Space Age' boots (made for wearing with mini-skirts) of the late 1960s. Top shoemakers charged very high prices for custom-made creations, but cheaper footwear, based on their ideas, could be purchased by almost anyone.

GLOBAL STYLES TODAY

Today, some poor people in developing countries still have no shoes to wear. Others, who work in traditional occupations like farming, still wear old-style boots and sandals. But in rich, developed nations, there is a wider range of footwear than ever before.

Moulded plastic ski-boots, with foam padding, nylon linings, and metal alloy bindings.

High tech

Today, people from wealthy nations take more holidays than their ancestors, and spend more of their income on leisure activities, such as skiing, hiking or diving. All need specialised footwear, for comfort and safety. Most leisure footwear is made of new synthetic materials, and relies on advanced technical knowledge.

Specialised styles

New technology has also helped develop footwear for all kinds of occupations. Deep-sea divers wear boots weighted with lead, fire-fighters have heatproof footwear, and electronics workers wear dustproof foot-coverings. Professional sports men and women also wear special boots and shoes. These can be difficult – and dangerous – to wear outside sports grounds. But they have inspired fashion footwear, from high heels to bedroom slippers.

Football boots have spikes, studs or curved blades fitted to their soles to give extra grip on wet, muddy turf.

Trainer power

Sports shoes, together with **sneakers**, have also inspired today's most popular footwear: mass-produced, brand-name trainers. These are worn by adults and children, for all kinds of activities, at home and out of doors. They are mostly made of synthetic materials, with cushioned soles and elaborate fastenings. New designs are made and promoted every year, to increase sales.

Trainers are decorated with their manufacturer's logo – an advertisement and status symbol.

What are the most popular style of shoes around the world today?

Sneakers.

Mix and match

For business, most adults in developed nations still wear sober styles: **laced** shoes or slip-ons for men, low-heeled **pumps** (plain fronted shoes) for women. Many children also still wear plain, simple shoes or boots for school. But on holiday, for parties, or relaxing with friends, adults and children can now chose from a vast variety of styles. Some are local and traditional; some are exclusive high fashion. Many blend designs or decorations from all round the globe.

Summer sandals, c 2005. Designed in Europe, manufactured in Asia, decorated in African, Indian and Native American style.

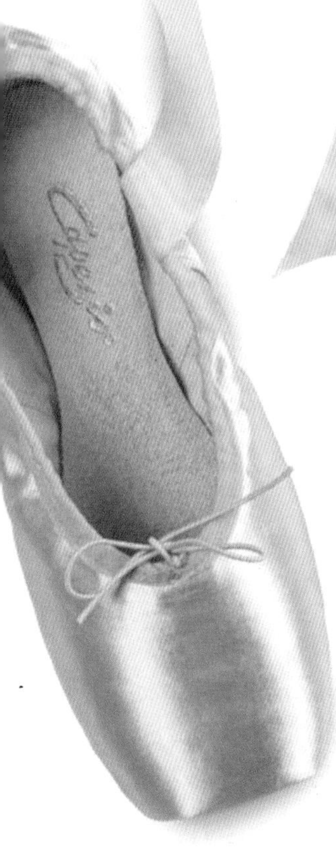

Ballet shoes designed especially to allow the dancer to stand on their toes

GLOSSARY/INDEX

afterlife Continued existence after death.

bark The outer layer of a tree-trunk.

bindings Fastenings that attach ski-boots to skis.

bovver boots Exaggerated version of workers' boots commonly worn in the 19th and early 20th centuries. After 1960, worn by rebellious young men in Britain. ('Bovver' = bother, or trouble.)

brogues Thick, heavy shoes, designed for country wear. Often decorated with stitches, punched hole patterns and tassels.

calcaei Leather laced shoes worn by wealthy roman.

caligae(plural) Boots worn by Roman soldiers. A single boot is called a 'caliga'.

clogs Thick, strong, backless shoes. Made of entirely of wood, or with wooden soles and cloth or leather uppers.

co-respondent shoes Two-colour shoes for men, fashionable in the early 20th century.

cordwainers Name formerly given to expert leatherworkers in Europe.

duck-bills Flat shoes with very wide toes, fashionable in the early 16th century.

erogenous Sexually attractive.

felt Thick cloth made from boiled, compressed wool.

gaiters Waterproof fabric leg-coverings (also known as spatterdashes).

geta Wooden clogs worn by women in Japan.

gorge Steep, narrow valley.

greaves Shin-protectors.

guilds Brotherhoods of skilled workers.

Hessians High leather boots, with a notch at the top of the shin, originally worn by German troops fighting in the USA in the 1770s and 1780s.

hide The skin of cattle and other large animals, such as deer or buffalo.

hobnailed Studded with metal nails, to give extra strength and toughness.

instep The top side of the foot, between the toes and the ankle.

kip-kap (also known as kub-kob) Wooden clogs worn by women in Turkey and West Asia

lace Thin strip of hide or leather, or narrow strip of braided thread.

laced Fastened with laces.

leather Animal skins that have been cleaned then treated (by drying, smoking or with chemicals) to preserve them.

leggings Leg-coverings made of woven cloth, knitted fabric, leather or sheepskin.

loafers Flat, slip-on shoes with a flat piece of leather covering the instep.

moccasins Shoes made of a single piece of leather, gathered around the foot, worn by Native North Americans.

mules Back-less shoes, with no covering for the heels.

Oxfords Smart, flat lace-up shoes, typically with four sets of holes for laces.

palm-fronds The long, thin leaves of date-palm and similar trees.

papyrus Reeds that grew in the River Nile.

pattens Mules with thick wooden soles, designed to keep the wearer's feet warm and dry. Sometime called clogs.

pomegranate A fruit with a yellow-orange rind covering many bright-red seeds surrounded by juicy pulp.

pumps Shoes with plain uppers and rounded toes.

sole The lower part of a boot or shoe, that touches the ground.

slashed Cut with tiny slits to reveal an inner lining.

sneakers Leisure shoes with rubber soles and cloth uppers.

spatterdashes Waterproof fabric leg-coverings (also known as gaiters).

spats Short, smart gaiters. Often side-fastening, with buttons.

tanned Coloured and preserved by soaking in chemicals.

tapestry Woven or embroidered picture or pattern.

terracotta Baked clay.

toe-post A short, strong strap on a sandal that passes between the toes.

udones The Roman name for socks made from woven material.

upper The top part of a shoe, that covers the foot.

Wellington boots Tall, straight-sided waterproof boots, first made for the British army commander, the Duke of Wellington, in the early 19th century.